# The Impact of a
# DIME

GERALDINE MORGAN

ISBN 978-1-68517-090-5 (paperback)
ISBN 978-1-68517-091-2 (digital)

Christian Faith Publishing, Inc.
832 Park Avenue
Meadville, PA 16335
www.christianfaithpublishing.com

Printed in the United States of America

I give God all the honor and glory, for without him, I can do nothing.

It is with great joy yet with sadness that I dedicate this book, *The Impact of a Dime*, to my mom—the late Mother Margie Boyd. She was my role model and prayer covering. She led by example, with a spirit of excellence and humility. My mom was a woman of few words, yet she had a great anointing.

So I thank you, Mom, for the impartation you spoke into my life that left an impact of me becoming the lady of excellence I am today.

# CONTENTS

# FOREWORD

I was six years old and bubbling with excitement. I stared out the window as I waited with much anticipation. *Today, I thought, I am going to have breakfast with Aunt Geri!*

When Aunt Geri arrived to pick me up, she was delighted to see me. I went with her to a particular destination. My experience was like that of Christmas morning. I was filled with excitement.

When we arrived at the location, I was stunned. She took me to the only place that would make any kid smile— McDonald's. When you're six years old, McDonald's is like dining at a Michelin three-star restaurant. Not only did we go to McDonald's but we went to the McDonald's mansion in Long Island, New York. There are only a few of these types of McDonald's in the US, so I was in heaven.

We ordered breakfast together and headed to get our seats. As I walked up the mansion steps, I felt like a king in a palace about to eat his supper. We finally sat down, ate, and talked. I expressed to her the busy life of a kindergartener.

This moment was one of the most memorable experiences I recall as a kid being with Aunt Geri. The only sad part about this experience was that she had to drop me off at school afterward. I thought, *Who wants to go to school when you have endless McDonald's available in a mansion with Aunt Geri?* I didn't want to leave.

As a grown man, reminiscing on my story, I realized how much that small moment of conversation and sharing with my Aunt Geri impacted my life. Simple words from a person of class and wisdom had an impact on my life. There is power in the small moments of conversation and sharing. There is power in words.

I'm reminded of the scriptures of Jesus and the centurion (Matthew 8:5–13). The centurion came to Jesus about one of his servants at his home who was paralyzed. Jesus told the centurion He would go with the centurion and heal him. The centurion stopped Jesus and said that he wasn't worthy to have Him in his house, but Jesus only needed to speak the word, and His servant would be healed. Jesus marveled at his faith, did as he requested, and the servant was healed immediately. Anyone in their natural mind will think, "Just speak a few words? But that's so small!" The centurion and Jesus understood what the author of *The Impact of a Dime* seeks to reveal to us, especially women from all walks of life. The author wants us to know that it's not the size of the gesture but the power of small gestures that can go a long way. When small words and gestures are shared, they can have a significant impact on the receiver.

In this book, *The Impact of a Dime*, it explores this very narrative as it takes you through countless examples found through the author's personal stories and the Word of God. This book is catered to helping women better understand how to build a relationship with their men.

Contrary to today's ideology where everything must be done in a great and grand manner, this book focuses on the big and small things. A small gesture of, "Hi!" can lead to a big smile. Small sunflower seeds can lead to a massive sunflower. Likewise, a small lie can lead to significant heartache, or a small leak can sink a ship.

Women often do not know much about the National Football League (NFL). However, many women play the game every day. Let me explain. There is a saying that goes like this, "Football is a game of inches." In *The Impact of a Dime*, it reveals how women can play the real-life game of inches, measured by how little she can provide to men and countless others to move them forward every day.

I'm confident that my few words will make a massive difference in how you think and approach this book. Remember it was a small act of kindness, in the life of a little six-year-old boy, that germinated a lifelong relationship of laughs, smiles, and sweet memories—powered through love. This little boy who is then honored to write the foreword for his aunt's second authored book.

I'm here to say this: This stuff works. Enjoy this book. Then go forth to share those small gestures and words and make a massive impact on others' lives.

Lovingly submitted from her favorite nephew and godson,

Joshua Boyd

Jamaica, New York

# ACKNOWLEDGMENTS

First and foremost, thank You, Lord, for Your unconditional love, mercy, and grace. You are my king and the very air that I breathe. I could never find the words or give enough praises to express my love and desire for You.

To my husband and best friend, Caswell Morgan, you are the one that holds the key to my heart. Together we have built a solid relationship where love flows, a home where we feel safe, and a family filled with love. Thank you for sharing my life, being my love, and helping make my dreams come true. You have encouraged me and inspired me to be all that God has destined for me to become. God created you just for me. My love for you will always be in my heart.

To my four children—Lora, Lance, Toby, and Dabari— you all are my joy and inspiration. You each have been there for me through thick and thin and my ups and downs. You are priceless and untradable! I say, "Thank you." You are all my cheerleaders.

To all of my grands and great-grands, you have Gigi's heart always.

A special thank-you to Earlene Campbell and Brenda Bonaparte for their clerical assistance.

Finally, to all my extended family and friends whom I love and appreciate, I say, "Thank you."

# INTRODUCTION

Many people might consider the value of a dime as insufficient, but adding it up can make a tremendous amount. One dime is only ten cents, a tenth of a dollar, but 1,000 dimes are one hundred dollars. The value of a dime increases as more dimes are added together.

There are slang phrases like "a drop of a dime" or "You aren't worth a dime." These terms tend to have negative connotations associated with them. However, there are favorable slang terms for a dime such as "dime piece" or "a perfect ten." I choose to share the aspect of a dime on a positive note.

The debate of small versus large or which is better is ongoing. People are always wondering, *Which is more powerful—small or large? Which carries more weight—small or large?*

I posed the question to several people, male and female, from all walks of life. I asked them, "Would you prefer to have a small dime or a large quarter?"

Unanimously, everyone I asked would proclaim, "Why ask that? Of course, the quarter."

People tend to naturally think that more is better or extensive, especially as it relates to money. Large represents more of any particular thing.

However, I would often reply to them, "Is the quarter really better? Is having more of something better?"

Let's think about this for a second. Does quantity, value, or size decide the true worth? Small can be stretched to become large.

In reading this book, you will discover how a dime becomes an umbrella in the storm of the lives of those connected to you. Whether it is a storm of health, family, death, or disaster, we women are dime droppers for men. We start fires in them. We have the power. Just a word or a sentence will help them with their questions of why. It can help them to hold on in pain, pressure, defeat, or persecution. After you drop dimes, destiny and purpose become one—they collide, and they can tell the enemy in the lives of men, "Game over!" Sharing a few words when they are facing pain, pressure, defeat, or persecution can become a life-changing moment for them. The Word of God admonishes us not to despise small beginnings (Zechariah 4:10, Job 8:7). So your words have power.

Someone may ask, "Do my words really have power?"

The resounding answer is, "Yes!" Your words have the power to cause action and produce an effect. It can possess or control, give authority, and influence others.

Let me share a short story told to me to help explain why your words have power. A pilot and a friend took a quick trip on the pilot's private plane. As the plane took flight, his friend sat super excited about the experience. Halfway into the flight, the pilot passed out, and the friend was now in charge of flying the plane.

Frantic, he began screaming and yelling over the radio, "Mayday! Mayday! I have an emergency!"

The words that came back after the explanation of the ordeal was this: "Calm down, calm down. If you listen to me, you will land the plane safely."

I say to women everywhere—words become powerful in an intense situation. There have been people in your life who have had many Mayday situations, but unbeknown to you, your words caused them to have a safe landing.

Anyone can count the seeds from an apple, but God counts all the apples that come from one seed. The dime you drop will help someone keep their hope alive. Men are waiting for you to drop a dime. They are waiting for you to drop wisdom to spark their passion and drive. Your dime can help them who are at the point of no return.

In this book, the dime represents designated assignments given to ordinary women who help everyday men become extraordinary through the drop of a dime—small words and gestures of wisdom and truth. These designated assignments often aren't recognized at first, but they are assignments that come from the Lord.

God knows how to arrange your life and footsteps to make you the answer to a problem or situation someone else is dealing with in their life. So remember this: Size does not dictate the power that something holds. You hold power. Speak your words—great or small, large or tiny. Drop those dimes. People are waiting to hear from you.

# CHAPTER 1

# THE FACE OF THE DIME

My name is Geraldine Morgan, also known as Geri, Lady Morgan, Mrs. Morgan, Gigi, Mom, and Auntie Morgan.

Being the oldest sibling with two sisters and two brothers, I encountered many challenges and obstacles. My parents, being God-fearing parents, instilled godly principles in me. These principles were a good foundation for me. I know today that God customized my life, and hence, I am a designer's original. With God's hand on my life and an assignment attached to my name, I understand now that it was inevitable that the devil had my name on his hit list. He set out time and time again to abort my God-given destiny and purpose.

As a woman, I believe I was defined by people and things that led me to lose sight of the original design God created me to be. It caused me not to acknowledge all the unique gifts and talents that were inside of me. I believed this was my truth but found it to be true of many women worldwide. They were defined by someone else, and this led them away from their true purpose from God.

My journey included red lights—warnings signs. When I should have stopped, I drove right through them due to a lack of knowledge of the Word and the right relationship with God. Immaturity, rebellion, and disobedience were all part of my journey. Then green lights told me to go, but poor decision-making caused me to turn down roads, leading me in the wrong direction. My flesh led me. The yellow lights that signaled me to slow down and stand still, I ignored and, instead, accelerated. It led to detours and dead-end zones.

Over and over again, I had questions that tossed through my mind. Questions like:

- Who am I? What am I supposed to do?

- Have I made a difference? Have I made an impact on anyone's life?

- Am I fulfilling a purpose? Am I walking in my destiny?

The process of getting the answers to these questions became very painful for me.

During many stages of my life, I was remade continuously on the Potter's wheel. He was molding and shaping me for the Master's use for an appointed time. I had to continually be remade because I kept getting off the Potter's wheel. When I got off the wheel, I had to deal with many things. I had to deal with a divorce, being a single mother, silently fighting through frustration and thoughts of suicide. Then there was the thought, *What will people say?* As a preacher's kid, there's always a label people put on us, and I had to deal with it. Thankfully I no longer wear that label. The victor in me now stands on what God says about me. After I got on the Potter's wheel for the last time, I allowed Him to work me all the way through until I was made to what He always intended me to be made of for His purpose.

I am the chief executive officer (CEO) and founder of Helping Desperate Women Survive (HDWS), Inspiration and Life LLC, and Life Jacket Savers, Inc. I have been called to inspire, motivate, coach, and counsel women from all walks of life. I am the life jacket for women by sharing my story to help save, change, and redirect their lives for the Kingdom of God.

At this stage of my life, I want to send a message of ageless passion to women everywhere. It's never too late! As I have become what God has ordained me to be, I am charged to ignite the fire inside women, to take them from being the victim to the victor. God has directed me to teach and inspire women who have lost hope, to teach and inspire women who feel defeated and feel like their dreams are no longer alive. Just as the Lord asked the prophet

Ezekiel the question in Chapter 37, "Can these bones live?" Well, through Christ, the answer is a resounding *yes*! I am evidence of this truth. I am alive and living to declare the works of the Lord.

I must share this with you: Never look at your age, background, or financial situation to step out of the box. It has held you in bondage for too long. God can take the little and make much when you put it in His hands. It's time to shut out the enemy's voice of negativity. Like my dad, the late Apostle John H. Boyd would say, I say it to you, "God can do more for you in five minutes than you can do for yourself in a lifetime." God has instilled greatness inside of you. There will always be battles on your journey that you must face. But if you avoid the battle you were born for, you will face another battle you are not equipped for.

Throughout my trials and tribulations, I learned to stay in my lane, stay on my mission, and avoid distractions. Distractions are the destruction. I learned to live my life in slow motion. I decided to live my life as an original so that I wouldn't die a copy. Hence I had to find my true identity through Christ.

I spent years in the trauma center with various diagnoses. When I was discharged, I didn't know how to apply the prescription of the Word. Thus I was always readmitted. But I was called and appointed by God with a purpose. He wasn't going to give up on me. When all of the props and masks of my life were pulled from me, the passion and gifts lying dormant became alive inside of me. My full attention was given to the Creator of my very being. My ears became attentive to His voice, and I became obedient to His call.

When God begins to strip away all of your props, makeup, and masks of life, you know He's cleaning and sanctifying you to demonstrate true beauty and purpose that can only come from Him. It's a wake-up call like no other. By way of the Word, a dream or vision, He will send confirmation that He's working on you. That's what He did with me. Yet I shake my head in regret of the wasted time I allowed to set me back from operating in the gift God graced to me.

As women, we often see ourselves as the weaker vessel, but God has put inside of us an exceptional endurance and perseverance. We are the wailing women on the walls that uplift and encourage the men that have been assigned to us. We shouldn't be unsure of how we have pushed others to fulfill their purpose and destiny. The Lord uses us to develop greatness in men of status. Sometimes we may not know it, but we often play an essential role in men's lives.

As for the men whose lives God allowed me to pour into, at first, I was not aware of the impact I was making. I was brought to tears from their testimonies. As a dime dropper, I had no idea that I was fulfilling my purpose and pushing them to fulfill theirs.

In writing this book, I am the face of the dime. I am a dime dropper. I am a woman who is God's chosen vessel to pour into others. I know who I am, and the God I serve is within me. As I have shared with you in this book, it is my endeavor that you, as women, know this: Never underestimate your worth. You are more vital and more valuable than you'll ever know. You, too, are the face of the dime. You are a dime dropper. Be the dime and drop those words of wisdom.

# CHAPTER 2

# THE RIGHT TIME

As a noun, *time* is defined as "the continued progress of existence and events in the past, present, and future regarded as a whole." As a verb, *time* is "a plan, schedule, or average when something should happen or should have been done." *Time* is also "the measured or measurable period during which an action, process, or condition exists or continues duration. Ultimately God is the definer of time. He is the controller of time. He is the eternal existence of the past, present, and future. He is whole. He is the planner and scheduler of all things. He knows what is to be done at the right time. Despite this truth, we have the option of how we use the time given to us.

We, as women, often transition into wearing so many hats during our journey. Throughout our life, we have many stages. First there is birth to age twelve. In this stage, we go from infancy to physical body changes. Then from age thirteen through nineteen, our mental development and decision-making skills develop. This time dictates the roads we will travel. From ages twenty through thirty, we tend to focus on our education, family, and career. By the ages of forty to fifty, we begin to question ourselves. We ask ourselves, "Who am I?" and "What have I accomplished?" As menopause begins, our body begins to change, and with it, so does our thinking. As we move into the next ages of sixty and over, many questions are being asked: What's next? Is it too late for me? Have I really made an impact on this world in any way? What do I have to show for my life? Will I leave a legacy?

There will be moments of pleasure in knowing that we have accomplished goals and had an impact. Music, pictures, movies, fashion, and conversations will be memories of joy and reflection. Then there will be a reflection on missed opportunities and open doors we never walked through.

The many life stages also have types of time that take place at each phase in some fashion. Let me explain these types of time.

- *Busy Time*

    These are moments we become involved in many areas of help. However, nothing is being accomplished during a busy time. It is full of things that help others but full of distractions leading us away from purpose. It's like being a jack-of-all-trades, and the master of none. It is trying to be everything, except one's self, to everybody.

- *Wasted Time*

These moments include being carried away in worldly activities and systems. Television shows and social media outlets like Facebook, Twitter, Instagram, Snapchat, or TikTok—these all become priority in our time. Then there is laziness, becoming a couch potato, shopping obsessions, and food indulgences. Let me not mention those rekindled lost friendships and relationships that are a total waste of time.

- *Productive Time*

These are times of obtaining knowledge and growth. Goals such as completing college, starting a business, or prospering in our career and family are the focal points of our life. Our passion pushes us to be productive citizens and continue productive activities, including reading books, networking, traveling, and gaining more knowledge.

- *Me Time*

These are times when we build our relationship with God. Spending time in prayer, eating healthy, taking a spa day, and even having a healthy exercise regimen. This type of time can also include creating a blog website, journaling, or doing something for others.

Time is a precious commodity. We cannot get it back. Once it's gone, we can only reflect on it. But from this day forward, we, as women, choose to use it wisely.

Now is the right time to be about our Father's business. Now is the right time—it doesn't matter what phase of life we're in and the time previously wasted. Today—it is time to go forward. No more wasted time with the past hurts of life. No more wasted time with unforgiveness. We now forgive—no more business as usual. We will be productive and will accomplish goals and even more goals because of Him that is within you and me.

Regardless of the phase of life you're in, you must be aware of time, as a dime dropper. You can be productive daily and use the gifts God has graced you with daily. Use time, each day, as if it was your last day on the Earth. Don't let distractions waste your time. They are time killers. As a dime dropper, it's not about how much time you have but, rather, about what you do with the time you have.

# CHAPTER 3

# FEARLESS WOMEN OF THE BIBLE

It is said that God uses ordinary people to do extraordinary things. One of the lessons we, as women, miss in life is this: We give dimes to everyday people who are on their way to becoming extraordinary through Christ.

We must be fearless and unashamed. We must say what God has given to us. We should not allow our self-esteem and feelings of inadequacies to cause us to miss opportunities or even share words with someone. The divine connections we have with ordinary people must be realized as they happen so that we can be in tune with what the Spirit wants to say, to take them as they're on their way to extraordinary. Note that at times, we may not know when a divine connection is happening, but nonetheless, we must always be in tune with the Spirit. He may reveal the divine connection in His time.

Reflecting on the year 2012, I listened to many touching life-changing stories from countless people during the homegoing celebration of my dad. It was mind-blowing. People from all walks of life spoke of how he helped them become who they now are—prosperous, saved, healed, and delivered. By way of a sermon, a counseling session, radio broadcast, hospital visit, or messages from the Gospel Tent, my father impacted the lives of many. He was a man of the public. The people of the community knew him. He often stood front onstage, not to be seen but to speak the truth.

On the other hand, in the year 2017, during the homegoing celebration of my mom, the late Mother Margie Boyd, there were testimonies of how she impacted the lives of many, but it was different. My mom was a woman of humility and integrity. She was soft-spoken, didn't preach a sermon, wasn't in the eyes of the public as often as my dad. Yet the testimonies of others let me know that she was a dime dropper. She often shared the friendly gesture of a smile or a few simple words. She dropped those dimes and propelled many to greatness, including that of the excellence of my father.

The question is this: How many times have we not dropped a dime to the one we were assigned to help? We can consider the one assigned to us ordinary; however, we should look at the extraordinary God has in them.

Take a look at those among you? There are some in your life who are ordinary but are on their way to the extraordinary through Christ. The men and family members of your life are waiting to hear from you. While you may be ordinary in your mind, you are a dime dropper and must drop them among the people of your life.

Many women of the Bible were good examples of ordinary women. However, they were fearless and spoke as they led.

As you continue to read about these women, understand their situation, understand their actions, and understand how God led them. Use these women to help you be fearless and speak to the extraordinary people among you.

## DEBORAH—WORDS OF THE PROPHETIC

After the death of Joshua, a woman named Deborah was chosen to rule over the Jewish people.

At this time, the Jews had turned away from the ways of God and adopted many idols. Due to their disobedience, God delivered them into the hands of King Jabin. He was cruel, and for twenty years, the people were oppressed. The Jews suffered under his reign, and in great despair, they cried to God. It was then that God sent them Deborah the prophetess.

Deborah resided in Ephraim, between Rama and Bethel, where sin and idolatry were in the midst. Despite this, Deborah remained faithful to God. Deborah stood firm to her belief in righteousness. She wanted the people of God to turn from their wicked ways. Her obedience to God allowed her to be a vessel of advice.

Deborah had favor and influence with even the strongest and novelist men of those days. This truth is noted in her experience with Barak. The scriptures say:

> And she sent and called Barak the son of Abinoam out of Kedeshnaphtali, and said unto him, Hath not The LORD God of Israel commanded, saying, Go and draw toward mount Tabor, and take with thee ten thousand men of the children of Naphtali and the children of Zebulun? And I will draw unto thee to the river Kishon Sisera, the captain of Jabin's army, with his chariots and his multitude; and I will deliver him into thine hand. (Judges 4:6–7 KJV)

God used Deborah to execute His plan on the Earth. He equipped her for this assignment.

Barack listened to the strategy Deborah shared with him. Yet Barack, secure in his own right, still revealed to Deborah his concern. He trusted her enough to reveal his weakness. The scriptures say, "And Barak said unto her, If thou wilt go with me, then I will go: but if thou wilt not go with me, then I will not go" (Judges 4:8). Barak understood that Deborah was anointed by God and desired her presence. "And she said, I will surely go with thee: notwithstanding the journey that thou takest shall not be for thine honour; for The LORD shall sell Sisera into the hand of a woman. And Deborah arose, and went with Barak to Kedesh" (Judges 4:9). As Deborah went with Barak and ten thousand men at his feet, the Lord granted His people victory at the hand of a woman.

As women, we may receive prophetic words from the Lord. Our responsibility is to release these words at the appointed time to men and others, when God permits us.

You have the Spirit of God in you to operate prophetically. You must allow Him to flow in you. Don't be afraid to be the voice of the prophet, to say, "Thus saith the Lord." The Lord used Deborah, and He can use you.

## MANOAH'S WIFE— WORDS OF INSIGHT

In Judges 13, we find a woman whose only identity was as Manoah's wife. She was barren, had no notoriety or popularity but would become the mother of Samson.

It was during the time of Judges when an angel of the Lord appeared to her. He told her that she would bear a child. She was given special instructions on what to eat. Also she was told that no razor was to touch the head of the son she was bearing. As the angel of the Lord was gone from her, she told her husband, Manoah, all of what the Lord told her. In his unbelief, he asked the Lord to send the angel that spoke these words. As the Lord granted him this request, Manoah's wife knew what was spoken of by the Lord. As Manoah entertained the angel, it wasn't until the angel of the Lord was gone from them that he realized that the Lord was in their presence. Manoah said, "We shall surely die because we have seen God" (v. 22).

It was at this time when Manoah's wife spoke these words; she said, "If The LORD were pleased to kill us, He would not have received a burnt offering and a meat offering at our hands, neither would He have shewed us all these things, nor would as at this time have told us such things as these" (v. 23). She knew she had received of the Lord. The insight of rational thought and understanding gave wisdom to the situation. Manoah's unbelief and own thoughts had him in the wrong direction. Her words steered him to the truth. Her words assured her husband that God's words were the truth.

You are often the assurance that men need to hear. You are the voice of reason and understanding. Sometimes they won't want to hear or accept the words you have, but you speak aloud and share the insight with clarity. Your words will lead him and others in the right direction to the truth.

## ABIGAIL—WORDS OF WISDOM

Abigail was intelligent and beautiful. She was married to a very prosperous man named Nabal, who was very foolish, brutal, and mean. Nabal's insult upset David greatly because David cared for Nabal's flock despite not knowing him or being asked to protect his flock. Because of this kind act, David commanded his army to travel to Maon, where Nabal lived, to request some supplies because of his kind act, but Nabal refused. The word of what happened between Nabel and David's men was told to Abigail by a young shepherd boy. He was aware of how powerful David and his men were and warned Abigail of impending disaster.

Abigail did not consider the boy's age or social status nor allowed him to be unheard. She listened to everything he said and quickly assessed the situation. Abigail allowed wisdom to take immediate action.

Abigail knew David needed supplies and food. She took loaves of bread, skins of wine, sheep, and cakes and loaded it on a donkey. She and her servants went out without saying anything to her husband.

Abigail bore the blame for the foolish actions of her husband. She fell to her knees, putting her face to the ground before David. Abigail spoke these words to David. She said:

> When the LORD has fulfilled my lord every good thing he promised concerning him and has appointed him ruler over Israel, my lord will not have on his conscience the staggering burden of needless bloodshed or of having avenged himself. And when the LORD your God has brought my lord success, remember your servant. (1 Samuel 25:30–31)

Abigail's wisdom showed David that it was not only her foolish husband's mistake not to honor God's anointed but also to show David that he should examine his character. She considered this: "When he would become king, he shouldn't want people to remember him for aimless bloodshed." David was impressed by the words of Abigail. He blessed the Lord that He sent her to meet him and gladly received her wisdom. Her words caused David not to shed blood. He received of her hand, which she brought to him and his men. Then he sent her away in peace (1 Samuel 25:32–35).

Abigail's wisdom brought her into the palace. Her willingness to show the Word of the Lord, at the risk of losing her life, caused her a promotion from being the wife of a fool to the wife of a king, namely King David.

Abigail's life is an example of God's promotion, and David was not intimidated by Abigail's wisdom. Instead, he celebrated her. Strong, confident women like Abigail do not threaten strong, secure men. Instead, they desire to have them in their lives and appreciate the wisdom they give to them.

So understand her example and speak wisdom. By detaching yourself from the world views of mankind and attaching to God's wisdom, you can dime-drop. You can cause war rumors to cease, cause the family argument to move to forgiveness, or cause suicidal thoughts to turn to thoughts of eternal life.

God has deposited dimes of wisdom in your mouth as women. When spoken at the right time to the right person, you become a recipient of promotion, which is not given according to location, experience, or education. Still it is a sovereign act of God.

## THE SHUNAMITE WOMAN— WORDS OF HOSPITALITY

In 2 Kings 4, we read about a woman of no name, who was ordinary—the Shunamite woman. In her experience, the prophet Elisha often visited and stayed at her home.

Because of his frequent visits, she spoke these words of hospitality to her husband:

> And she said unto her husband, Behold now, I perceive that this is an holy man of God, which passeth by us continually. Let us make a little chamber, I pray thee, on the wall; and let us set for him there a bed, and a table, and a stool, and a candlestick: and it shall be, when he cometh to us, that he shall turn in thither. And it fell on a day, that he came thither, and he turned into the chamber and lay there. (2 Kings 4:9-11)

Those words of hospitality she spoke to her husband caused his seed and her womb to come alive at the word of the prophet. She was barren, but her husband listened to her kindness. God ultimately saw her kindness, and Prophet Elisha spoke into their lives, and they conceived a son in their old age (vv. 16–18).

As a group of women, it is essential to know how to capture the moment. The Shunamite woman knew how to seize the opportunity with dimes of hospitality because she recognized a man that had a connection with God.

God will allow different men to have access to our lives. The kind words and actions of hospitality will meet a need in their life but activate the fulfillment of a desire in our life unbeknown to us. Whether it be a child, job change, healing of relationships, or finances, when we allow hospitality to flow from our hearts, it causes the dead areas of our life to be resurrected.

# RUTH—WORDS OF RESOLUTION

As I have shared in this chapter about women of the Bible dime-dropping to men, not all of our dime dropping are for men. Let's understand the experience of Ruth.

Ruth was a Moabite (Ruth 1:1–22). She was a part of a nation that worshiped the false god, Chumash. Ruth was married to Mahlon, who was of Hebrew descent. His mother, Naomi, and father, Elimelech, had come to Moab from Bethlehem because of a famine. While there, Mahlon married Ruth. His brother, Kihon, married Oprah, who was also a Moabite.

Moab was considered a cursed place. They were worshipers of idol gods, and for Ruth, this spiritual atmosphere of idolatry was all she knew. Despite Ruth's past, God had a plan to use her in a way that impacted history.

After some time, Elimelech, Naomi's husband died. After that, Mahlon died, and so did Kihon. Here was Naomi, a Hebrew woman, living in Moab, with two daughters-in-law. They all found themselves alone in the world. They were at the end of choices with no real way to change their circumstances. According to their culture, without a man, they had no alternative to help them out.

With no real thought of hope, Naomi purposed to return to her homeland, Bethlehem. Naomi told her daughters-in-law to return to their family and homes. She was a woman who could have remarried and bore sons to give to them, but they would have to wait years before they could marry. So Naomi sent them away.

Ruth already had a life full of despair. She could have felt like a victim and could have thrown in the towel and left Naomi. But Ruth had to have known that Naomi was a good woman. This statement must be valid, for Ruth spoke words of resolve, decisiveness, and conclusion. "And Ruth said, Intreat me not to leave thee, or to return from following after thee: for whither thou goest, I will go; and where thou lodgest, I will lodge: thy people shall be my people, and thy God my God" (Ruth 1:16). While Oprah returned to her family, Ruth was determined to follow Naomi. She connected with Naomi, who was related to God, which caused her to decide essentially to accept God over Moab's gods. Ruth's decision to go with Naomi allowed Naomi to understand her desire to be with her and stay committed to her regardless of the situation.

Upon Ruth's acceptance of God over gods, she came to Bethlehem with Naomi and found favor with Boaz. He was kind to Naomi. They later married, and this marriage led to Obed's birth, the great-grandfather of David, which was of the lineage of Jesus Christ. Her resolve to be with God allowed Naomi to accept her words, which then blessed Ruth with everything that she lost back at her home. She gained it all because she decided to stay with God.

We should not be indecisive in our truth, to speak it and live it. When we speak, we must be distinct, purposeful, and resolve to tell the truth. The hearers will understand and know our resolve to live by the truth and support us in living the truth. At the same time, God will bless us for living in the truth. Let us resolve to follow the example of Ruth and follow after God.

# HANNAH—WORDS OF CORRECTION

It's not what you say at times but how it is said.

Hannah was barren for many years. Every year, when her husband, Eli, went to the temple to offer sacrifices, she would go and pray in the temple. During one visit to the temple, Hannah went in to pray. Amid Hannah's prayer, the priest, Eli, was watching her. He thought she was drunk as he was not able to decipher her words.

The scriptures say:

> And it came to pass, as she continued
> praying before The Lord, that Eli marked
> her mouth. Now Hannah, she spake in

her heart; only her lips moved, but her voice was not heard: therefore Eli thought she had been drunken. And Eli said unto her, How long wilt thou be drunken? put away thy wine from thee. And Hannah answered and said, No, my lord, I am a woman of a sorrowful spirit: I have drunk neither wine nor strong drink, but have poured out my soul before The Lord. Count not thine handmaid for a daughter of Belial: for out of the abundance of my complaint and grief have I spoken hitherto. Then Eli answered and said, Go in peace: and the God of Israel grant thee thy petition that thou hast asked of Him. (1 Samuel 1:12–17)

Hannah did not flip off in anger or hatred to the man of God. Instead, she spoke softly with grace in her sorrow and through her pain.

A soft word of correction goes a long way when dealing with men. We are wise in our approach not to cause anger but to cause truth to be heard.

By Hannah's soft, gentle words, Eli, the priest, understood that God was at work. He blessed her. Her character in this situation only allowed God to work in her favor the more. The Lord answered her prayer and granted her a son,

Samuel, who later became the prophet who would anoint David as king.

# RAHAB—THE ACT OF KINDNESS

Rehab, once a prostitute, later became the mother of Boaz and the great-grandmother of King David. She lived in Jericho when the Israelites were taking over the land of Cannon at the mighty hand of God.

During this time, Rehab gave shelter to two Israelite spies. Rahab took the initiative in declaring her faith in God by an act of kindness. Truthfully, she lied when she said she saw the spies go another way, but her truth was this: God's hand was at work, and her act of kindness was her truth. Her truth allowed her life and the life of her family to be spared.

Before Rahab's great deliverance, her future seemed to be helpless, hopeless, and one of destruction. She was an outcast and was left destitute, with no way to provide for herself. God has a way of dealing with woman with a past. Like Rahab, God still has a use for us women who may have a history, have told lies, and have even done worse things than Rahab.

We must live in our truth—that God uses women to impact men of destiny. We know that all things work together for good. Like Rahab, God will use us women with a past.

The act of kindness you do in your truth will lead to blessings and the greater good. Don't let your past deter you from your truth and destiny through Christ.

# ESTHER—WORDS OF COURAGE

Esther was an orphan raised by her uncle Mordecai. Esther had no desire to be a queen. She desired to live her life quietly in peace as a Jew. She had no desire for riches or fame. She did not have her eye on greatness or on changing the world. But destiny came into action.

When Esther was chosen as the new queen of Persia, it was then that her assignment became clear to her. Her promotion could have gone to her head. After all, her beauty was confirmed by the king. She was considered the most beautiful woman in the land. But Esther soon realized there was a more excellent reason she was given this assignment as queen of Persia.

Esther found herself facing a difficult situation. Esther learned of Haman's decree to kill the Jews of the land. This decree wouldn't spare the life of the queen, for Esther was a Jew as well. So Esther did the unthinkable. She took courage and went to the king without being summoned. If you were not summoned by the king, anyone approaching, including the queen, would be struck down.

Mordecai urged Esther to use all of her influence to change the king's deadly decree. So she said in Esther 4:16, "Go, gather together all the Jews that are present in Shushan, and fast ye for me, and neither eat nor drink three days, night or day: I also and my maidens will fast likewise; and so will I go in unto the king, which is not according to the law: and if I perish, I perish." She knew it was necessary to be courageous and rely on the Lord to guide her to do the right thing for His people.

Life does not always go as we think or plan. We are often put into positions we didn't ask for but must handle. Nevertheless we must be like Esther. We must be courageous in the midst of confusion. We must not allow our human nature of fear to cause us to be deterred from the courage we have in Jesus. So we must speak up and stay true to gestures of peace and truth. If we perish, we perish.

These examples of women of the Bible were ordinary women who were fearless. They could speak and perform gestures of kindness, correction, hospitality, wisdom, and truth.

As women and dime droppers, we must learn how to approach all of mankind to impact their lives. A small act of kindness can lead to an open door. A word of encouragement can lead to someone's ability to overcome. We may think of ourselves as small or ordinary, but we are extraordinary. We are fearless women.

# CHAPTER 4

# ME? A DIME DROPPER?

As I've stated before, as women, we often will not always know that the words and gestures we share with various people will have a considerable impact.

I was offered the opportunity to hear many testimonies from several men to whom I've had the pleasure of impacting over the years. It is a blessing to know that I could share a friendly gesture or words of wisdom into the lives of the men who have come into my life.

As women, many of you may not have the opportunity to hear others' messages regarding how you've impacted their lives. So if the chance never avails itself, don't be hindered from continuing to be a dime dropper. Forever stay faithful to God and His Word.

# LUKE SANTIAGO

My name is Luke. I used to be a student at Bethel Christian Academy (BCA). During my time in BCA, Mrs. Morgan had impacted my life tremendously.

During one of the darkest moments in life, Mrs. Morgan was a warmhearted woman, and—overall—a fantastic person. She was always comforting, when talking with me. She was the emotional support I needed to overcome the challenges I was facing at that time.

During the month of October, in the year 2012, Hurricane Sandy hit New York City. Specifically, this hurricane had a great impact on those living in Far Rockaway, Queens. My house flooded during the storm. I thought I would die, as my family and I were in the house while it was flooding. We were in one room watching, as the water level grew higher and higher. It was a traumatizing experience. I couldn't get any sleep that night, but luckily, we got to escape. Once we escaped from the house, we were forced to leave the place that provided us with so many wonderful memories and live in a shelter in Queens, New York.

Now living in a shelter, the horror continued. I wouldn't wish it on my worst enemy. The shelter was crowded and unsanitary. It was the longest week of my life; it was the epitome of hell.

Through the darkness, there was light, and that light so happened to be Mrs. Morgan. After missing many weeks of school, I was welcomed back with open arms by Mrs. Morgan. Mrs. Morgan genuinely cared for me and made a considerable effort to help me in my situation. It was the little communication; talking helped me cope with my depressive state of mind. I felt like Mrs. Morgan was always going to be there when I was in a dreadful situation.

Mrs. Morgan is a very accepting person. She understood that life doesn't always have positive outcomes. But even though life doesn't always have good outcomes, there are still people like Mrs. Morgan who help others to get by. I often think about how my life would have been like without the positive impact of Mrs. Morgan. If it wasn't for her, who knows how long it would've taken for me to get out of that depressive state.

I want to say thank you, Mrs. Morgan, for all the positive and beautiful memories of my life.

## TYLER ELMORE

There have been endless times in my life where I can think back and remember when I had hit a rough point, and out of the blue, I'll get a text from Gigi. The one I remember most is right before I started my first day of camp for my freshman football year. I was so nervous. I knew I was good enough but didn't know what to expect and didn't know how far behind I would be being a true freshman.

The night before my first day, I got a text from Gigi that said, "Praying for you. I know you can do this, and most importantly, you know you can do this." That text meant so much to me. It just reassured the belief that I belonged and could compete. Gigi always seemed to send me a text or give me a call when I needed it the most. I'm truly blessed to have her in my life, and thank God for her every day.

# ROBERT JONES

I could write forever about how my life changed through meeting Lady Morgan's father, the late Apostle John H. Boyd. I had the opportunity to live in his basement for over six years. He loved me like a son.

I've always looked up to Lady Morgan. She is a true woman of God. She always had that big sister effect on me from the first time I met her. She's always giving me encouraging words that would make my day and inspire me to keep going with God and stay in my word—the most outstanding advice.

There's one specific memory I have that I want to share. On Sunday, April 27, 1997, during the 8:00 a.m. service, Dr. C. Morgan was preaching. The Holy Ghost was working so strong through him during the whole service. Toward the end, Dr. Morgan was laying hands with people all over the floor. Then she got up and started to lay hands on people. She was laying them down in Jesus's name, with people all over the floor. The Apostle Boyd came in with Prophet A. Jones and me as his armor bearer, and she looked at me and said, "Brother Robert, run down here, right now!"

I ran as fast as I could, and she laid hands on me over and over and over again until I couldn't stand anymore. She said to me, "You will give my testimony all over the world. From the east to the west, from the south to the north."

I wrote those words down in the first Bible Apostle Boyd gave me. I still have this Bible. I will show it to you one day.

You are a great example of Proverbs 31:10–27. All women—young and old—can learn from Lady Morgan, not only women but men too.

# "IT TAKES A VILLAGE" BY DEANGELO WILLIAMS

Growing up in a cross-cultural environment leaves a prepubescent, alpha-male child confused, aggressive, and, sometimes, downright disrespectful. That's just the start of it. Issues at home, arguments, changing of religious beliefs, seeing the lack of knowledge of my, at that time, uninformed parents were things I regularly dealt with during those teenage years.

After spending a year homeschooled by a mother who saw my intelligence, I was left to teach myself. Now let me remind you again—I was going through puberty, cross-culturally confused, having issues at home, changing my religious beliefs, and lacked structure. Yet I was left to learn on my own.

Now take me—this confused young teenager—and enter me into a school for the first time. At BCA was where I was introduced to Mrs. Morgan, who was the assistant principal of BCA.

Entering the Bethel Christian Academy—Bethel as we called it—I entered into my tenth grade with some eleventh-grade classes. During my orientation, the assistant principal kept looking at me. As she did, my greatest fear set in. I said to myself, *Did I date her daughter?* Luckily that wasn't the issue. Later I learned that she kept looking at me because I reminded her of her oldest son, Lance.

During orientation, I automatically put my defense up. Slowly but surely, I released my defense and began to visit her office, and I came to know her as Lady Morgan.

During my hectic days at school, I found comfort and peace in her office. The environment was always pristine; all the papers were neatly stacked, books placed in the right place, and the colors were always calming, soothing, and made me feel like at any time, warm, hot cookies can appear out of nowhere. Although it didn't, there was always candy on your exit.

Lady Morgan is a woman of class, style, and poise. She has a unique ability not to say a word while you explain your situation. Her ability not to say a word often made me wonder if she was listening. But trust me, I learned that she was listening. Her line was always, "Okay, are you fin- ished?" This statement meant this: You are about to get the cold, hard facts. She would explain where I went wrong, show me where others may have gone wrong, and say it's always about how I handle the situation. I remember her specifically saying, "Everyone gets angry. If you keep your peace, the other person looks crazy. It takes two to fight." This advice was one of the best pieces of advice I had ever received during my teenage years.

Being the great student I was, I always tried my best to apply what I learned. One day, as an adolescent teen, my great and wise mother decided she wanted to argue with me. But you know, I'm an adolescent; I'm always right, remember? At that moment, I applied the sound advice I received from Lady Morgan. As all amazing West Indian parents do, my sweet and loving mother began to go for the jugular. The wisdom of Lady Morgan set in. I heard her say in my mind. "Don't say a word, D (DeAngelo)." So I simply watched as this West Indian flail her arms and point at me. I listened to her tone and volume but didn't say a word. Somewhere in the middle of the pointing and the accent, I laughed—which only made the situation worse for me. Her advice really worked for me and allowed me to realize that sometimes, saying nothing (and not laughing) is the best thing I could do in situations.

Advice and comfort flowed from her; the wisdom and kindness overflowed in many areas of my development. There's another example of her wisdom I can remember clearly. I remember it so well because I still have the scar on my hand. There was this beautiful girl—four feet and eleven inches, Cherokee black goddess; she had a fantastic cheekbone structure, full lips, and a beautiful body. As an eleventh grader, what more can I ask for in a future girl-friend? I liked her, and it was clear. I purchased her roses and chocolates. I would walk her to her van, and I even convinced my parents to put me in the same van she came in to spend more time with her.

Unfortunately, the frequency of my attendance at Lady Morgan's office increased. Lady Morgan and I sat in her office, trying to figure out the complexity of this woman. I asked what to do and how to do it. I asked her what to say and how to say it. I asked her should I stay or should I go. Lady Morgan wouldn't shy away from the hard questions. I recall her asking me, "Did you have sex with her?" Luckily I didn't, but she was that beautiful that I couldn't let anyone else date her.

After multiple conversations with Lady Morgan and several appeals by her for me to stop involving myself with this girl, that one day after math class, the beautiful Cherokee came up to me and said, "I'm sorry for upsetting you."

I replied, "You have to stop talking to me like that."

Somehow that translated to something else in her head. This young Cherokee—all of four feet and eleven inches—decided that at that moment, she was seven feet, two inches and placed her pointer and middle finger to the temple of my five-foot-ten stature and verbalized loudly, "I will do what I want!"

As she mushed me in the head in front of the entire class, in harmony, they all yelled, "Ooooooooooohhhhhhhh."

Bruised ego in hand, Lady Morgan's voice in my head said to me, "Leave that young lady alone." These words overpowered the instinct to wrap my hands around Cherokee's neck. I, instead, addressed the onlookers in hopes not to excite her. I turned to the crowd and said, "Don't hype her!"

Before I was fully finished with my sentence, she did it again. She mushed me and said, "Now what?"

After that, I blacked out. My fist tightened, jaw clenched, and eyes focused on the part of her jaw I was going to make a connection to. Time slowed down. The consequences of my action passed through my mind. The thought of the pain I was about to cause the young woman also passed through my mind. The disappointment that I would cause my family passed through my mind, but strangely enough, the voice of Lady Morgan saying, "I told you to leave her alone," caused my hand to reposition itself to the blackboard nailed to the wall. I struck it with such force that the bone that runs from my knuckles to my wrist broke on impact. I needed surgery, including rods, to hold the bone in place while it healed.

After the ordeal, I remember my classmates telling me that the hole was on display for a whole month.

On my return to school, I was ordered to Lady Morgan's office. I hope to be comforted and consoled. I walked into her office, and she said, "How stupid are you!"

In my mind, I said, "Wait! What?"

She continued, "You have to be the dumbest person I know. Why, DeAngelo, why?"

After a pause of silence, she said, "I bet you learned your lesson now?"

She went on for about a minute, and nothing she said was wrong. I took all that she said into my heart. I knew it came from a place of love and genuine care for my well-being.

For the next few months, Lady Morgan would see me in the hallway and shook her head. When I tried to visit her, she would not allow me in the office. In my heart, I believed it was because she didn't want to see me hurting. It was her expression of love.

# Ricardo James

The impact one's life has on another isn't measured by the length of time but the impression's quality.

There have been many times when "the quiet storm," as I call Lady Geraldine Morgan, has made a long-lasting impression on my life.

I've never told anyone this, but there is one moment that stands out most when Lady Morgan left an impression on my life. This impression occurred at a pivotal time in my life when I silently struggled with confidence in my calling and my ability to make a difference.

My heart has always been grounded in the idea of using my God-given gifts, talents, and abilities to serve humanity. My professional background is in fashion and visual merchandising, and I always wanted to create something to give back to the youth and young adults in my community. I partnered with my then church to create a fashion, art, and leadership program called Fashion House Academy (FHA). It was geared toward youth and young adults ages eleven to twenty-one, giving them hands-on, creative education and the opportunity to explore professions in the fashion and arts industry. My church donated space for us to have our sessions. We used the classrooms at their Christian school in the evenings. I reached out to my friends in the fashion industry, who agreed to give their time and talent to come once a week and instruct classes for our students.

The FHA program was a hit and operated successfully for four years. We received publicity from CBS News and 1010 WINS, their nationally syndicated radio broadcast.

We partnered with the Police Athletic League (PAL) of Queens, New York, to host a beta program called "The FHA Cadets." We also worked with community officials in Far Rockaway, Queens, New York, to host and supply clothing for their annual community day events. We were growing. Then everything came to an abrupt stop. Partnerships didn't work out; student attendance declined; instructors pulled out; and the church's space was no longer available.

Everything was changing. I didn't know how to shift. I was blaming myself for all of the changes. I took the blame for it all in my emotional strain.

Because FHA was my brainchild, everything was personal to me. I decided to shut the program down. I felt like a failure. I felt like I failed my kids, my program, my community, and my calling.

Word had gotten to me that Mrs. Morgan was working on a project and wanted a meeting with me. I've always been known as a resourceful guy and consulted with people all over the world, so I thought this was just another consulting opportunity. When we met, she asked me if I could help plan and host her school's annual fundraising benefit dinner and fashion show. Immediately it reminded me of the things that pulled my heartstrings—using my gifts and talents to help youth and young adults in my community—but it also reminded me of my self-proclaimed failure with FHA. It was tough for me to decide if I would help because of my internal pride and struggle. After I fought through my gang of emotions and insecurities, I agreed to help.

Now here's a caveat. As simple as this was, the conversation Mrs. Morgan and I had impacted my life on so many levels.

Here are some lessons I learned through this conversation:

- Failure doesn't decrease or erase your value. Although I thought I failed miserably, that was just a feeling. The reality was I took a step of faith to start the program, and that was already a victory. Every student, instructor, parent, and volunteer that served with us only had a recollection of the memories we created and not the moment we closed. Those memories and that experience added a tremendous amount of value to their lives and my own.

- One opportunity will lead to another. I thought FHA was it. As dramatic as it sounded, in my mind, no one would ever ask me to participate in any fashion-related program or event involving youth or young adults because FHA closed. When Mrs. Morgan asked me to be a part of what she was doing, it showed me that there was still demand for my ability, and when one door closes, another door of opportunity in another area will open. It wasn't even about the size of the role; it was the simple fact that I was being asked to be a part of a team and project, doing something near and dear to my heart.

- People are watching your life. I believe we focus more on being perfect when others are watching rather than being authentic. Life isn't always about just the win. Sometimes it's the process of loving something enough to commit to seeing it through from one phase to the next, even if it's not long-lasting. In that moment of authentic love and commitment, there is a beautiful quality that develops without regard for an end in sight. And it's that quality and others alike that attracts others to your life.

Mrs. Morgan and I had never spent much time together personally, but she had seen my diligence and hard work consistently, through many different platforms and opportunities over the years. She looked at me and didn't see what I saw, which was a failure at one thing but saw success at many different things. She gave me an opportunity.

Can you imagine the wealth of knowledge and experience someone who has failed brings to a team? They can identify potential blind spots in a place where others can't see because they haven't fallen in that area. I felt like she saw that and recognized the value I brought to her team, and I am forever grateful for that moment we had that built my confidence and restored my faith in my calling and ability to make a difference.

# ANDRE JONES

When someone inspires, an impact is left—an impression, a deposit, and not a withdrawal. Inspiration can be both overt and covert, but they both accomplish the same results. When I looked into the origin of the word *inspire*, Webster says it comes from the Latin *inspiratus*—the past participle of inspirare, which means "to breathe into, inspires."

When I think of my aunt Geri, "Mrs. Morgan" as I call her, there are two words that readily comes to mind—excellence and inspiration. Everyone that knows her knows that she is a woman who believes in excellence. No matter what task is in front of her, she always aims to complete it in the spirit of excellence. Whenever you know you would be working on something with Mrs. Morgan, you knew you'd better bring your A+ game.

Her example has inspired me to continually reach for excellence in all that I do, both in ministry and business. She has shown not only to be an inspiration to me but to everyone that connects to her.

I've not only had the privilege to admire her from a distance but also up close. As a kid, my younger brother and I would always fight over who would play with one of our favorite cousins, Toby, Mrs. Morgan's youngest son. No matter what, we loved going over to our cousin's house in Suffolk County, New York. Not only did we have a great time being three high-energy boys, but when you walked into the house, Mr. Morgan always had the house looking immaculate. Nothing ever seemed to be out of place! This was an authentic example of what it looked like to have a virtuous wife and mother who took care of her home.

Whether it was in her personal or professional life, she's always been an example of excellence and a source of inspiration. Today those two attributes, which are persistently at the cornerstone of anything I do, were inspired by watching it in her life.

Greatness is not always about words, but many times, it's also about presence. There were times, unbeknown to her, I'd sit in Mrs. Morgan's office, not clear on something I was dealing with, or I was simply there looking for inspiration. It was at those moments that I'd find answers and inspiration by merely having a listening ear.

One of my favorite quotes, by an unknown author, is this: "The word *listen* has the same letters as the word *silent*." There were many times that, in her silence, I'd find a great listener! I'm thankful that God allowed her to impart into my life and become an intricate part of who I am today!

# LANCE ELMORE

I cannot remember my mother carrying me in her womb or the first time my eyes saw her face, but my heart does. There is no recollection of her rocking me to sleep when I cried in the middle of the night nor her nursing, cuddling, or singing to me, but my heart remembers. There is no memory of the first time she said my name or her holding my hand or sitting on her lap, but my heart—it remembers. I can't remember her first prayer over me or the sound of her voice reading me a book, but my heart knows and remembers.

See, there are so many things I cannot recall, but I know, my heart and soul—it knows. The things I cannot remember are what shaped me and guided me, and as I grew older, they often sustained me. Her love, her faith, her prayers, and her strength—over my life, these things have helped sculpt who I am. From the moments and events I can't remember to the ones that are seared in my mind, my mother has been an intricate part of my life's blueprint. In storms, in uncertainty, at the lowest of valleys, and amid dark days, I could count on my mom and her unyielding faith to speak into my life and reassure hope. Distance has never hindered my mom's ability to love me or impact my life. Her love and faith are not deterred by physics or geography. Circumstances or momentary trials do not sway it. My mom moves mountains with her faith and speaks love in my heart, regardless of what may come.

There is so much I don't remember, but I know my heart knows, and who I am today proves the greatness of the woman I call mother. I'm grateful that she loves me unconditionally and gives me so much in my life.

# "Dime Dropper" by Toby Elmore

In sports, a person who drops dimes is usually doing something spectacular or making an incredible feat.

We often don't equate the same greatness to those who drop dimes in our lives with those who drop them on the basketball court or the field. The spectacular and astounding feats performed receives high praise. For example, during a regular-season game of 2017–2018, LeBron James of the Cleveland Cavaliers threw a beautiful, no-look pass against the Los Angeles Lakers. The pass was remarkable; it was replayed over and over throughout the rest of the regular season. LeBron dropped an incredible dime that will be spoken about for some time. While this feat is seen by many and spoken about, there are the amazing feats of a dime dropped within a life that go unnoticed until shared.

I would like to take this time to say that this magnificent dime dropper has been dropping dimes for years; none of which has been seen on ESPN Top Ten.

Geraldine Morgan has done her share of dime dropping, not dimes like LeBron, Kobe, MJ, Brady, or Rodgers, but she has dropped priceless dimes in the lives of those who came to know her. Lady Morgan, as she is affectionately known, is a beacon of positivity and love. Her heart is one that is filled with God's purpose and plan. To drop this type of precious dimes, for them to be useful, practical, and substantial, a person's heart has to be right with God. Lady

Morgan has a right heart with God, for she has been able to drop precious dimes.

I have had a great perspective and opportunity to see this fantastic dime dropper at work.

When she turns out to be your mother, and you have had the experience of watching and receiving from her, you realize how special and blessed you are to know that God made it part of His plan to touch your life in so many ways, even though it was only a dime. Yet to know that the dime that was imparted to me turned into dimes and has brought about wealth to my life is priceless.

The questions that came to mind as I reflected on my mom were: What is a dime? How was it delivered? What made it a dime? How has it changed my life or anything for that matter? I found many of the answers to these questions through her. Let's take a look and see.

For something to warrant a story or a classification, I believe it needs to have shaped or shifted a part of your life. The delivery methods will be precisely what they need to reach you at the time and place you are at in your life. What dime did Lady Morgan, Mom, drop on me that changed the course of my life? What she shared was direct and straightforward but carries across every facet of life.

She said, "In this great world we live in, with all its freedoms and liberties, you are free to choose your path, your road, your destination. Toby, you have freedom of choices, but always remember, you do not have freedom from your choices' consequences. The Bible says you will reap what you sow. So in everything you choose to do, consider the cost."

Major dime drop. Powerful life lesson.

This statement has held my entire life. I teach this principle; I pay this dime forward to friends, coworkers, students, and players that come across my path.

If applied during your decision-making process, you will find just how much counting the cost will help direct your choices.

In a world of instant gratification and the search for pleasure, a dime statement like this tends to slip through the cracks. However, I am eternally grateful for all the dimes I've been blessed to receive and collect from her. I am also honored to share them with many others, to pay homage to the gestures and words she's given to me.

After many years of me simply being me, reading comments from other people regarding my dime dropping was a blessing for me. I didn't include these testimonials to pat myself on the back. I added these testimonials so that you can know that even if no one ever comes and share their experience of you dime dropping, you continue to dime drop.

As dime dropping can simply be you being an example, having one conversation with a person, sharing your life with a person, or simply being a voice of counsel, dime dropping is valuable and must be done.

Our reward is in heaven. What we do and say should not be predicated on what we get in return. We must do and say only because of the Spirit of God within us.

So dime drop and share with others. Don't be hindered by your hindrances and insecurities. There is someone who needs to receive your dime. It is valuable. It is precious. It is needed. It is to be shared.

# CHAPTER 5

# THE STOLEN DIME

*In all thy ways acknowledge him,*
*and he shall direct thy paths.*

—Proverbs 3:6

"The Stolen Dime" is a story that will have you rethink what seems insignificant can become a life changer in someone's life. It brings to life how words on a card impacts the life of a total stranger with a crossroad decision to make.

## "THE STOLEN DIME" BY CARRIE LARSEN

I hope by the time you are reading this in print, the word *pandemic* is a word from our distant memory. At the time this story happened, it was late fall of 2020 when the onset of pandemic life was in full swing, and finding things to be joyful about was limited to watching a Hallmark Christmas movie that I had not seen yet.

The spark came early on a Saturday morning in November that today was the day I am going to decorate for Christmas—Christmas brings me joy, and I needed joy to fill the house in this strange way to end the year. You can probably relate that decorating for Christmas has its highs and lows. The high—when finished and seeing everything decorated, but the lows come when you think about the boxes that need to be pulled out from storage. It's a mixed bag, as you can imagine. Outcome—the decorations, and off I went to the big box store to gather a few things I need to make the decorations and tree complete. Can you sense the joy and pep in my step as I share how this adventure begins?

Part of the excitement is where the events of this day expand. In the big box store, I shopped and got my loot of goods, headed to the register, and out the door I went, excited to get home and start the Christmas remodel. I got home, grabbed my purse, and quickly realized my wallet was missing. Fear and tears flood my emotions as I head back to the store, chanting prayers to God that it would be found. Anyone who has gotten their wallet stolen knows that everything, and I mean everything, is in that wallet—credit cards, gift cards, ID, passport ID, loyalty cards—everything. My search at the store came back empty-handed, and I felt deflated and all the excitement I had escaped me like a pierced balloon. As I drove back home, I knew my excitement and joy from getting the decorations had me blindsided to being careless about my wallet; the mental beat-myself-up game was in full affect. I made the numerous calls to report my cards stolen, and the day progressed with the Christmas remodel not even in sight.

I wouldn't say this is my lowest point in life, but I would say that I was feeling pretty low. I had no money, no cards to get money, no ID to say that it was me who wanted my money from the bank. I had nothing—so I thought.

What I have learned over the years of walking with God is oftentimes, when we walk in the valleys is when God gives us what I call *God squeezes* to remind us that He holds us in the palm of His hand. A little squeeze to remind us that even though we walk through the valley, the mountain peak is right around the corner. A little squeeze to remind us that everything is going to be okay.

Squeeze one came from a close friend hearing about my wallet being stolen, who offered to give me money to get groceries. *Wow*, what a blessing. Okay, God, I see you working, and off to the grocery store I went. Being a non-cash-carrying person, I brought with me $40, thinking that would be enough. I loaded the cart up, got in line, and panic set in—my items in the cart now seemed well over $40. I told Sabrina the cashier that I may need to go get more money because I didn't bring in enough. She laughed behind her mask and glanced at my items left in the cart and said, "I think you will make it."

I jokingly replied, "What's your over or under for $40?"

Again she laughed and she just continued to scan the items. I didn't think she realized the panic that was building deep within. As each item was scanned, the amount owed rose, and we hit the goal with about six items remaining in the cart. As the last item was scanned and the amount due to well over $40, Sabrina glanced over at me and told me not to worry about it, that she will pay for it. Sabrina shared that over the years, when she needed it, people helped her, and she felt this was a time to pay that forward and help me. Stunned and in shock, I thanked her over and over again. As I walked to my car, a few tears welled up in the corner of my eye, knowing that this was another God squeeze, and I accepted it fully. Even as I am typing that sentence now, it brings me back to that day and am so thankful that God has got me. He knew I needed that affirmation.

Fast forward to Monday, my wallet had been gone for three days, and for the most part, life has moved on. New cards were being ordered and sent; new ID was ordered, and the sadness has dissipated—a new week was starting, and a new outlook was had.

I began to finish that goal of decorating for Christmas. The star was placed on top of the tree, and the nativity was on display. It was perfect. The day progressed quickly, and Monday night at around 9:30 p.m., my phone rang with a local number that I didn't know. The mental debate began—*Do I answer or not? Who would be calling this late?*

and more importantly, *Who is this calling that is not in my contacts?*

Going against my usual behavior, I answered the phone. As the gentleman introduced himself, he shared that he was the manager at a local clothing store. He stated that I had left my wallet at the store while shopping there today. Confused because I had not gone to this store on this day or the days that preceded it, I confirmed that it was indeed my wallet and asked when I could pick it up. The store was closing, but he was willing to wait for me to come over and pick it up that night. I felt the God squeeze as I put my shoes on and dashed over to the store. I thanked the manager, and as I shared the story of how and when it was stolen, the excitement and joy overcame me. I could no longer put the words together. I got back in my car and quickly thumbed through the wallet to realize that every card, every gift card, every receipt, every loyalty card was, indeed, still in my wallet. The word *wow* was an understatement to how I was feeling at that moment. Thoughts of where my wallet had been, who had it, and the conversations that took place around my wallet flooded my mind. What made the thief return the wallet to a different store fully intact was my greatest thought. After a few joyous phone calls to share the news, I went to sleep contemplating those exact thoughts.

Tuesday morning, I woke up with a little extra pep in my step. Receiving the blessing of having my wallet back and beginning the process to reorganize my cards in the slots, it dawned on me, staring me right in the face, my scripture card that was behind the plastic clear view slot was there. The scripture card was that of Jeremiah 29:11 that states, "For I know the plans I have for you," declares the Lord, "plans to prosper you and not to harm you, plans to give you hope and a future." At that moment, I knew with confidence what conversations happened around my wallet those three days. A conversation with God. A conversation with God and someone who had stolen my wallet. A conversation with God reminding the person who took my wallet that God has plans for them. That it was the moment to make a better decision—a different decision than they would normally make. A decision that would allow God to prosper them in a way that they could not imagine. It was in reading this scripture card that I realized that my low of losing my wallet and the tears and lesson that came from that was not for my growing purpose, but it was for someone else's. The greater blessing was that this unknown stranger, for a moment, read God's word and, in my mind, had a conversation with a King about how there is a better life to be had and how making this decision to not keep the wallet and not even use the gifts cards but to return the wallet fully intact would allow this person to receive the blessing that God declares for each of us. Now that was a goose bump God squeeze, and I loved seeing how God works in mysterious ways and not just God working but allowing my low to be used for God's good, and to that, I say, "Amen!"

# CHAPTER 6

# DIME—DIVINE INTERVENTION MOMENTS OF ENLIGHTENMENT

As I pinned this book, I felt the need to ensure that you fully comprehended the concept of *The Impact of a Dime*, which turned out to be an acronym—DIME.

*Divine* is defined as "a form of the likeness of God." It is used to describe something related to God. This word is the best word to describe the gestures and expressions that we women, as dime droppers, share with others. What we do comes from God. As believers, everything we do in word and deed must be done in the spirit of love.

This love is not like that of mankind but that unconditional love that comes from God. He demonstrated His great love for us when He sent His own Son to die for our sins. As our prime example of the divine, we must follow

His example. As Jesus did on Earth, we must follow Him and do as He has done.

We must keep our hearts attuned to what the Spirit is directing us to do and say. We mustn't be about our business. We must be about our Father's business.

*Intervention* is defined as "the act of becoming involved." *Intervention* means "to come in between two things." We are set out to come between darkness and light. We are to come between the darkness that men often go through and lead them to light. Our acts and words are divine but healing in nature. Our intervention is in relationships that stop a disaster, save lives, and speaks life.

Moments are brief periods which can occur in an instant or extended point of time. As a support system to the men who have been assigned to our lives, we provide comfort, security, and advice in moments. Sometimes these moments can be long-term, as we see this occur in our marriages, friendships, and other relationships with people we see and speak to daily. At the same time, these moments can be onetime moments of contact with people. Hence dime moments are pivotal and can occur at any time. We must stay on guard and be ready to speak peace and truth at the drop of a dime.

Enlightenment is the effect of the cause of dropping the dime. The act of spiritual truth and impartation of knowledge or a gesture causes men to connect with God through us. It allows them to put down their thought of hatred, disaster, or whatever they're going through and see the Lord through our dime dropping.

The divine interactive moments of enlightenment shared with men are powerful. The women of the Bible propelled many men forward to countless victories through Christ. Likewise, there is a great cloud of witnesses who have gone before us. If we hear their testimonies and accounts of the many words and gestures they gave men at the most vulnerable times of their life, we, too, will be reminded of the power we have.

If we connect and know that the Lord values us, our women's instinct—the inner voice of the Lord will work through us. We will save lives and stop disasters by merely speaking a word, sharing a story, smiling at someone, or a friendly gesture.

The Word says in Proverbs 3:6, "In all thy ways acknowledge Him, and He shall direct thy paths." When dealing with DIME, the best place to start is by the acknowledgment of Him. This acknowledgment will require that we begin with Him in prayer daily. It's a daily morning necessity that we need. We know not who has been assigned to our lives for that day, so we must pray.

I've had moments during the day when I was compelled to speak words of life to someone or do something I usually wouldn't do.

Don't despise the little statement you share, such as "You look like a winner," or "You look ready for this football season." Don't let small statements keep you from speaking up. Go with the flow. At that moment, that man might be pondering the decision of suicide, drugs, divorce, or quitting a job. Our words or sentences could cause a beam of enlightenment to shift his atmosphere from negative energy to a positive outlook.

As women, we will experience times of enlightenment as well. We could be compelled to have an interest in something we've never had a claim with before. For example, if you become interested in the basketball playoffs, if this happens, it could be God trying to teach you something, at that moment, to help you have a DIME moment with some young man later.

In another case, you may take the bus to work and give the bus driver a keychain that says, "God loves you," which reminds him that he is loved. Furthermore, don't let the idea of doing something you may hate to do—like bake cookies—keep you from doing it. The cookies you share to someone could remind them that someone is thinking of them.

As one plants and another waters, it is God who gives the increase. As a DIME is meant to be the planting and watering, we as women play a role in participating in them both. The words and the gestures turn men back to God.

As women, we throw ourselves under the bus as insufficient and of no value or worth. Yet we are dime droppers in the lives of so many men. God created us and downloaded inside of us the instinct, creativity, and wisdom to bless them. We are the walking women of prayer.

Men are under pressure, have insecurities, and have the need to be encouraged and strengthened. God knew this, and He created a woman. God said in Genesis 2:18, "It is not good that the man should be alone; I will make him an help meet for him." We are the helpmeet of men. We are torch carriers. We are dime droppers.

# CHAPTER 7

# Don't Sell Yourself Short

Take a long look in the mirror. Who do you see?

You are wonderfully and fearfully made from the hands of the Creator. Inside you is a warm heart full of love and kindness. There are words of inspiration that rest in the inner chambers of your soul. They are waiting to speak through your mouth to a little boy, teenager, young adult, middle-aged male, or maybe some senior citizen male. We know men are strong, challenging, and altogether, but you are among the many women around this world set to encourage, motivate, and propel men to their destiny.

Dime dropping is a gift God has placed in women, as a part of our instinct and senses. So our soft-spoken words, passing smile, or gentle hug break shackles and break the mental depression that often lay hidden in men.

Yes! Yes! Yes! Just one word, a few sentences, maybe even a paragraph, or a story—any of these can turn their life upside down and cause them to realize their worth.

The impact you did not see or might never know is that the dime or dimes that you shared on common grounds on an ordinary day are times that leave meaning with others. You thought the gesture or words to be very insignificant, but it was powerful.

While dropping dimes, you will ask yourself, "Why did I say that?" or "Why did I share that?" There will be conversations that cause you to ask, "Why did the conversation take a right turn on a subject that seem to have no relevance to them in anyway?" But those moments are God-ordained. They are driven by Him to cause you to dime drop. It was already predesigned for the exchanging of paths for you and that man to meet.

Dimes have a way of sending a message. I received a dime message in the wee hours of the night. I watched a movie on television, not realizing that it was about to confirm my writing this book. The movie was about a couple who went away on a short trip to regroup after their young-adult son's tragic death. It was something that they hadn't prepared for nor expected to happen. As they knew he was taken away from them too soon, they reflected on the life that could have been if their son was still alive. They continued to battle the question of *why* during the movie, until they went into their son's room. Once they entered the room, there on the bed was his laptop, and when they lifted it up, out fell dimes. Specifically, they didn't know why he collected them and stored them, but they realized that he valued them enough to keep them. They were able to move forward in their life remembering their son every time they saw a dime. The significance of a dime transformed their lives forever. I thought, *Wow!* There was a connection with the story and my purpose with this book. As I reflect on that moment, I don't even remember why I was awake at 3:00 a.m. and watching television. Yet it was powerful to see the connection of a movie about death, opening a laptop, and dimes dropping out. As the tears streamed down my face, it was this small dime—a movie— which confirmed my purpose with this book.

In the movie, the dime symbolized their son's love and his presence.

Through this book, I pray that you've come to realize that the dime represents the power of words and gestures.

I speak to all the women out there today: Don't sell yourself short! Stop feeling insignificant! You think that because your name is not in lights, not on a billboard, or that you don't have a ton of social media followers that you are not significant. But inside, you have dimes that have so much power in provoking a great man. God will use these dimes in different ways to change and make the world better.

As a predator waiting to attack, you don't know if the person is a karate-black-belt holder; similarly, most men don't see that you are a dime dropper waiting to impact their lives. You can't sell yourself short. You have it within you, but you have to know it and follow through with it. Don't sell yourself short!

# WOMEN
# DIME DROPPERS

In our mouth are dimes that were, that are,

That will shape and design men;

Men of all ages, colors, and from every walk of life.

So, women—sound the alarm.

Think not of yourself as less than,

Think of yourself as more than conquerors.

Inside of you—unbeknown to you—

There is the antidote to weakness,

The opposite of discouragement.

You can uplift,

You can redirect paths,

You can redefine their mind-set;

You can help men assigned to you.

You, Me—We are dime droppers.

We're saving lives at the drop of a dime.

We drop dimes on the street,

At the beach,

On the job or even at the mall.

Riding on the train, bus, or the plane,

We are dropping dimes.

There's no time of day—

Morning, noon, or night—

When they are not falling from us.

We are imparting them everywhere.

We are dime droppers.

We embrace our calling.

We embrace the Father.

We know our purpose.

We share our purpose.

We go forward as dime droppers.

*The Impact of the Dime—*

We drop them fearlessly.

We know that it will produce.

We know that it will heal.

We know it will prosper.

Become a cheerleader for the small things. The Bible lets us know not to despise small beginnings. As we journey in life, we must not forget that it takes preparation to excel in the future. God starts us out with the small things. Don't pass up the opportunity to help that man or boy because of their status or your feelings of insufficiency. Never feel your act of kindness, smile, or words of encouragement do not have an impact to someone's life.

# CHAPTER 8

# ISSUES MEN FACE

This chapter brings to light various issues men are confronted with during their lifetime, which can lead to silent frustration. The appearance of being strong, self-sufficient, showing no emotions, and the I-can-do-it-all syndrome continues to paint a picture that represents a false reality. After reading this chapter, I pray, as women, that you come away with a better understanding of the impact that is needed from you for the men which are your assignment.

- *Burnout Syndrome*

  Men may be pressured into feeling they must take on everything or become addicted to approval, which will cause burnout. Many times, they spend their lives making other people happy, at the expense of never being happy themselves. Burnouts can result from the lack of discernment or because of unwarranted guilt. Eventually they will develop silent frustration.

- *Lack of Confidence or Fear*

Fear can be like a virus. It starts as a thought but starts to affect his emotions and behavior. As a virus feeds the body, a man who is fearful has no confidence and can never reach his potential in life. Fear is a cruel ruler and keeps him in constant torment. Fear paralyzes faith. Fear is a plague with a silent war in his ear gates.

- *Anger*

We all have become angry at one time or another. Yet there are men and boys who become angry frequently. This may be due to a root of being insecure. They often find themselves easily offended by others. They must be treated well in order to feel good about themselves. When this spirit of anger remains locked inside, it allows the enemy to manifest through bitterness, resentment, and unforgiveness. Men will often fly into rages where their emotions will become out of control. Anger causes the mouth to work faster than the mind.

- *Patience*

Men of God who have been given assignments face many challenges or warfare. Therefore, much patience will be required. Many times, men are in the stage of zeal, with the lack of knowledge. Some are not yet prepared for the assignment. Remember it took forty years in the wilderness for Moses. There are those who think purpose and destiny are like microwaves. They forget that patience is a virtue.

- *Quitting*

  Life can become very overwhelming for men, especially when things seem to be going upside-down in the wrong direction—when the bills are piling up; pressure on a job or at home; various twists and turns that come unexpected. Yes, they struggle with "I want to quit."

Men and boys face struggles and challenges of different types in their lives. Many times, as women, we fail to note the inner emotional status of men. We must remember they are not creatures of emotions like we are. To the man that is in a season of burnout, just share three words. Learn to say no.

To the man that wants to quit or throw in the towel—let him know that if you quit today, you will never know what lies around the corner. Quitting is not an option!

To the man that lacks patience—patience pays great dividends that you cannot begin to imagine.

To the man who has anger—send him an emoji with a smile, or simply say, "God loves you!"

To the man that is fearful—send him a picture of a lion or just say, "It's time to roar!"

We are the fuel for the men God has assigned to us. They are like a plane on the runway with no fuel—they have the potential to fly high but cannot get off the ground. They need us to drop a dime.

# CHAPTER 9

# IS YOUR FACE ON A DIME?

Our responsibility as dime droppers doesn't stop throughout our lives. So it's essential to not cut ourselves short because of our age, culture, background, education, and past experiences. We have the power to heal the land with the dime we have to share.

## IMPARTATION

The means to which we impart dimes to men and others can occur in three ways. It includes how we speak, how we act, and how we see them.

- *How We Speak*

  "Then was our mouth filled with laughter, and our tongue with singing" (Psalm 126:2a).

"He will yet fill your mouth with laughter and your lips with shouts of joy" (Job 8:21 NIV).

"Strength and honour are her clothing; and she shall rejoice in time to come. She openeth her mouth with wisdom; and in her tongue is the law of kindness" (Proverbs 31:25–26).

How we, as women, speak to men is one of the primary means of dropping dimes. Of course this could occur in wisdom, through counsel and personal testimonies. A critical aspect of how we speak is humor.

The humor of a story or funny incident that could be shared can lift a depressed man. Proverbs 17 says, "A cheerful heart makes good medicine." Life is better when people are laughing. So don't feel uncomfortable sharing a joyful or an embarrassing personal story that causes someone to smile. You won't look silly or be put to shame by your experiences that brought laughter to someone else.

Humor can be shared through movies, stories, or pictures. Laughter opens up feelings for one to express what is truly going on.

- *How We Act*

Next we can impart by putting actions behind the word we speak. One act of a smile, a hug, card, or gift can impart to any man in need. Many men of God have come into my life that depicted characters and qualities of negativity and depression, but I was able to act in kindness, a hug or gift, which turned things around in their life.

Some of you, women, have unique talents with food, sewing, poetry, hospitality, and other talents. These gifts and talents are to be used to impart not only to those you live with but also something that can set peace in the hearts of men who you do not know.

- *How We See*

The way we see men are often dictated by the men who raised us. The presence or lack of a father in our lives, as we were being raised, could have implications on the men we marry and father our children. Furthermore, the interaction of men or boys during growing pains will also impact how we see them. Yet the relationship we have with the Father and how He sees men in the Word helps cultivate and correct our views of men.

The experiences we had with men that hurt us can all be healed once we give our lives to our Heavenly Father.

I've realized over the years that I've always seen men differently. When society, culture, the government, or any other group saw fearfulness, I saw boldness. They saw indifference; I saw compassion. They saw rashness; I saw consciousness. They saw underachievement; I saw creativity. They saw inconsistency; I saw dependability. They saw a quitter; I saw endurance. They saw apathy; I saw enthusiasm. They saw rejection; I saw forgiveness. They saw harshness; I saw gentleness. They saw loneliness; I saw hospitality. They saw self-pity; I saw joyfulness. They saw selfishness; I saw love. They saw anger; I saw meekness. They saw disorganization; I saw orderliness. They saw wastefulness; I saw resourcefulness. They saw unreliability; I saw responsibility. They saw anxiety; I saw security. They saw self-indulgence; I saw self-control. They saw incompleteness; I saw completeness. They saw impurity; I saw virtue. They saw inclination; I saw wisdom. They saw hypocrisy; I saw sincerity. They saw callousness; I saw sensitivity. They saw disrespect; I saw reverence. They saw self-centeredness; I saw availability.

As women, we are strong in word and deed. It is crucial that we do not drive back from hearing and being obedient to God and what He wants to connect us to, whether the man be a family member, coworker, CEO, celebrity, the rich and famous, or the homeless man on the street. Fear not what you say to them, for fear doesn't come from God.

He has equipped us with everything we need to impart to those who may appear to be strong, but we are awaiting the dime dropper to drop a dime into their hearts.

Many times, we have no idea the dilemma or issues men are faced with. They just might be on life support, and God uses you like a defibrillator to revive them back to life. It is not the big things that makes a difference in life, but it is the unnoticed and small gestures that become life changing.

I charge you to be BAD—*b*old, *a*nointed, and *d*etermined. By sharing, you bring peace to that man in any atmosphere, whether it is in a room, prison, hospital, or car. Remember you are the life jacket for the person who is drowning in deep waters. You are the lifeline God is using to rescue them. You are not inadequate to make an impact. You are the life jacket connector to rescue that man. You have the strength of a lion inside of you. There is a giant that surpasses the spirit of your feeling worthless.

Conquer that challenge or obstacle! Rise and go forth to impact! Notice that ordinary can become extraordinary when you do not allow failure to be an option.

# ABOUT THE AUTHOR

*Passion is ageless. Tell your story, and*
*become a life jacket for others.*

—Geraldine Morgan

Geraldine Morgan is a seasoned inspirational speaker, author, and mentor.

She is happily married to Dr. Caswell Morgan. She has four children, Lora, Lance, Toby, and Dabari, and is a devoted grandmother and great-grandmother. She has strong family values that are exhibited in her daily life.

In working diligently by her father's side, the late Apostle John H. Boyd Sr., founder of the New Greater Bethel Ministries, Geraldine has operated in her gifting of leadership and administration. Through her father's experiences, she learned to apply faith with demonstration, which is now exhibited in her daily walk with God. Her mother, the late Mother Margie Boyd, inspired her to operate in the spirit of humility, with an excellent spirit.

After thirty years of service in education administration for Bethel Christian Academy, Geraldine progressed to full-time ministry. She is presently on staff at the New Greater Bethel Bible Institute, as an instructor of women's agenda, a course that discusses the Bible and being a woman in a sinful world.

Geraldine is chief executive officer and founder of Inspiration and Life LLC, Life Jacket Savers Inc., and the nonprofit organization, Helping Desperate Women Survive. She is the author of *A Treasure of Lifesavers for Victorious Living* and host of the web series *Life Jacket Connections*.

Geraldine has been awarded various citations of appreciation for her dedication to humanitarian services.

Geraldine is a designer's original. She represents the balance of dedication to her home, church, and outreach ministry. Her wisdom, knowledge, integrity, and steadfastness have enhanced her ability to become all God has designed for her life as a dime dropper.

CPSIA information can be obtained
at www.ICGtesting.com
Printed in the USA
BVHW091321290522
638419BV00001BD/71